Dedicated to Sahib Jora's Naniji and Nanaji,
loving grandparents who are passionate
about their faith.

Sikh
FUN-damentals!

Written by: Minnie Rai-Manhas
Illustrated by: Svetlana Lau

I'm Jind Kaur,
and I am a Sikh.

A Sikh means *learner.*
I love to learn new things.

Sikhi teaches that everyone is equal no matter gender, race, disability, class, or creed.

Humanity is one.

My parents give both me
and my brother the same
love and respect.

When I meet my Sikh brothers and sisters,
I greet them by saying *Sat Sri Akal.*

Sat Sri Akal means God,
or *Waheguru*, is Truth.

Sometimes I also greet them
by saying *Waheguru Ji Ka Khalsa!*
Waheguru Ji Ki Fateh!

That means the Khalsa
belongs to *Waheguru*, the Victory
belongs to *Waheguru*.

Sikhi teaches 3 important ways to live a meaningful life.

Naam Japo, Kirat Karo and Vand Chhako.

Naam Japo
means to meditate.

I like to meditate with my family.

Sometimes I go to the gurdwara
to meditate with the *sangat*,
or congregation.

It makes me feel calm and good inside.

Kirat Karo means to live honestly.

Everyday I watch my parents
work hard and live honest lives.

They teach me to always
do the right thing!

Vand chhako means to share your time, talent, and wealth with others.

Food Bank

Every Sunday my parents,
brother and I donate groceries
and canned goods to our local food bank.

We also go to the gurdwara to do *langar sewa*. *Langar* is served at all gurdwaras and is a free vegetarian meal for everybody!

It is made and funded by the Sikh community.

I like going to the gurdwara because I also see my friends there.

We like to do
sewa together which
means to selflessly serve others.

My friends and I like
to hand out parshadey
to those eating langar.

Sikhi teaches so many valuable lessons.

Being a Sikh is fun!

Glossary

Gurdwara — means the "Guru's house" or the "Door that leads to the Guru", or commonly understood as the Sikh place of worship where Sikhs are meant to congregate, pray, and learn together as a community.

Guru — 'gu' = darkness and 'ru' = light. It refers to the light that dispels darkness through the form of the ten Sikh Gurus (teachers/masters) and Waheguru (God).

Kaur — princess, a last name used by Sikh women to abandon traditional surnames that would denote caste. Men use the last name Singh, meaning lion.

Kirat Karo — one of the three pillars of the Sikh faith that instructs Sikhs to live an honest and pure life.

Langar — is a community kitchen introduced to help nourish everyone regardless of faith or caste and symbolizes that everyone is equal as it is a free vegetarian meal eaten on the floor. It is served at all gurdwaras. It is operated and funded by the Sikh community who volunteer their time and resources to ensure it is successfully run.

Naam Japo — one of the three pillars of the Sikh faith that instructs Sikhs to be in constant remembrance of Waheguru.

Parshadey — rotis or round-shaped unleavened bread.

Sangat — refers to community, and in the Sikh tradition represents the congregation coming together to help uplift each other through prayer and good deeds.

Sat Sri Akal — is a greeting that Sikhs say to each other with hands in prayer pose. It means that Waheguru is Truth.

Sikh — a learner or disciple who is constantly learning and following the teachings of the Guru.

Sikhi — is the term to correctly describe the Sikh faith as opposed to the commonly used Sikhism.

Sewa — an important practice for Sikhs to always selflessly serve others without expecting anything in return.

Vand Chhako — one of the three pillars of the Sikh faith that instructs Sikhs to share the fruits of their labour with others, especially those in less fortunate positions.

Waheguru — means wondrous teacher, and is a term commonly understood as God.

Waheguru Ji Ka Khalsa, Waheguru Ji Ki Fateh — a salutation used by Sikhs, especially those who have taken Amrit, or commonly understood to be baptized. Literal translation means the Khalsa belongs to Waheguru, the Victory belongs to Waheguru.

Made in the USA
Las Vegas, NV
27 May 2024

90458076R00017